Brainstorming session

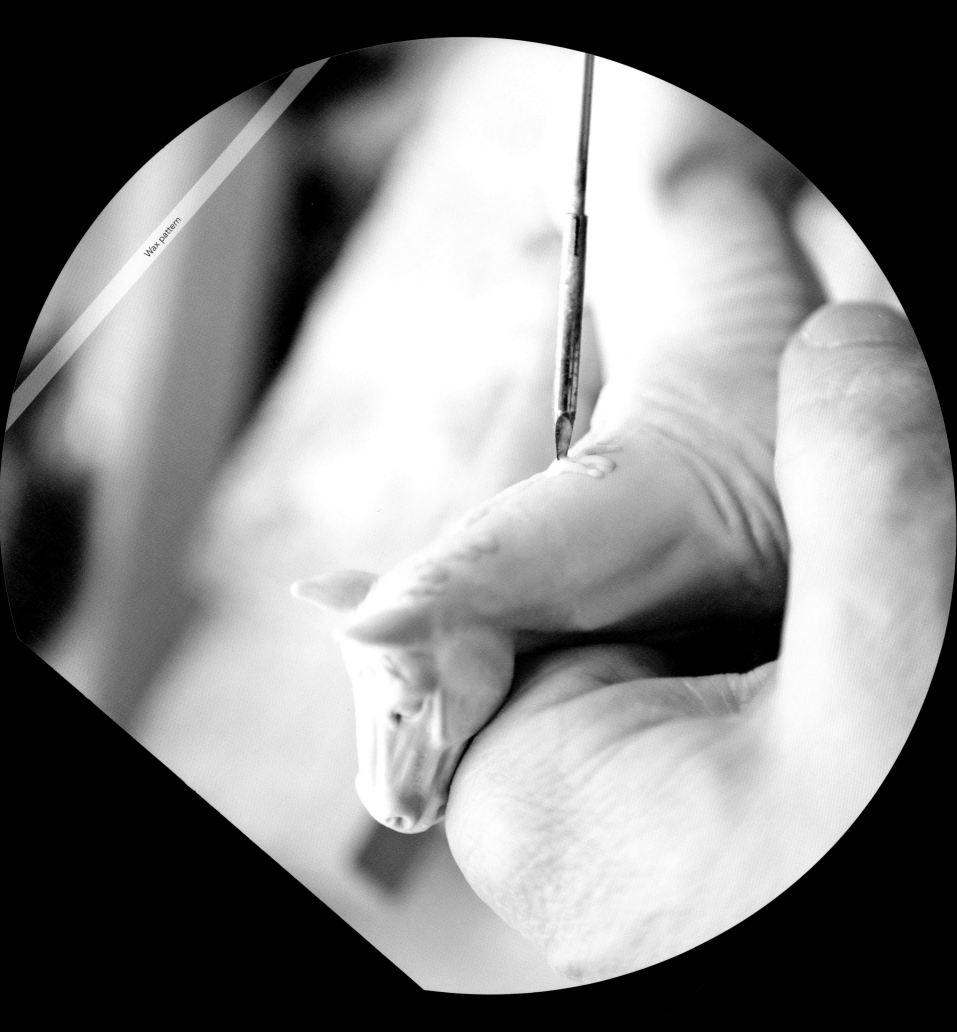

Wax pattern

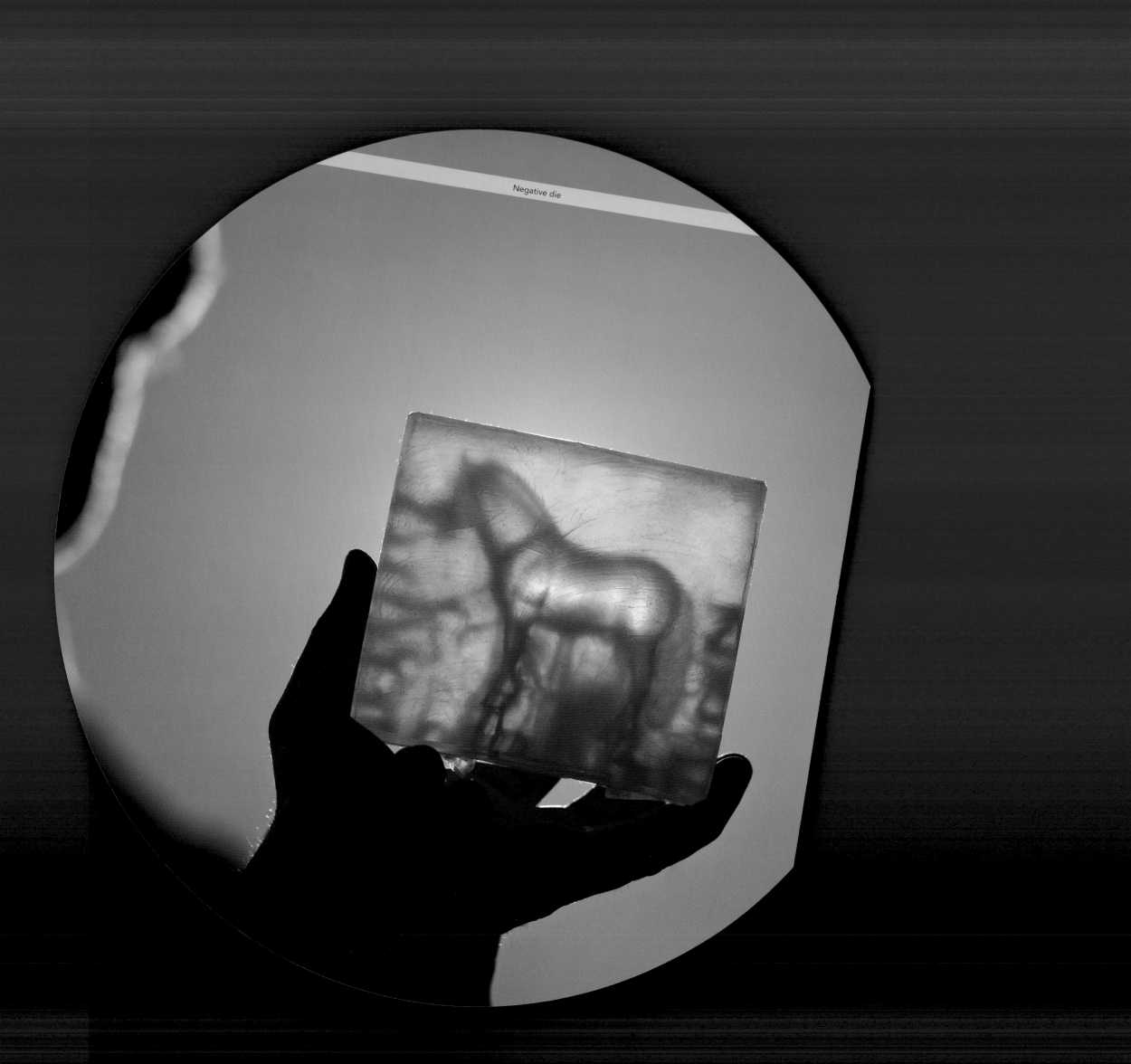

Dressing the resin pattern

Waxing up the die

Plaster mould

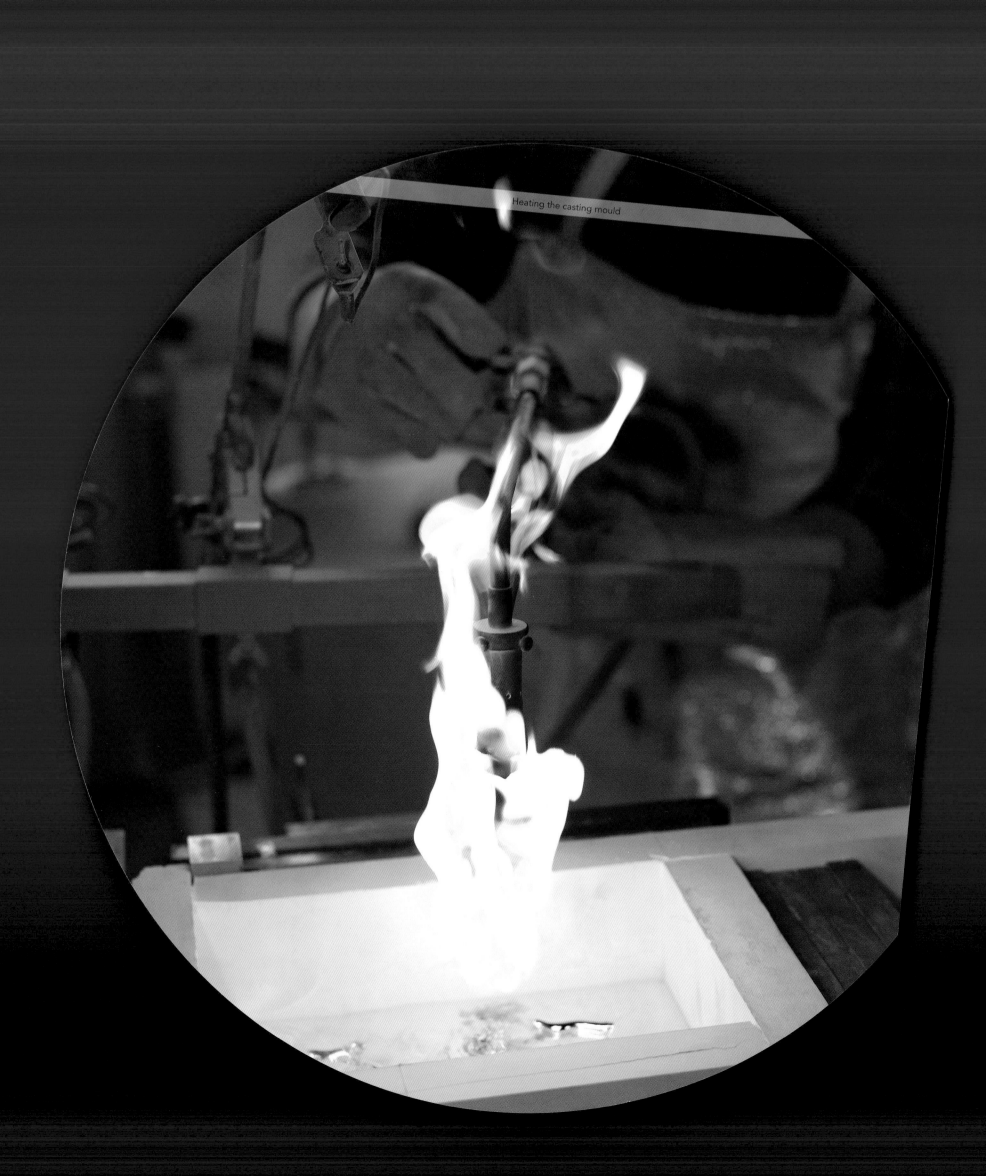

Heating the casting mould

Fine-tuning the casting mould

Mixing the colours

Cold water bath

Imaginative Play

"Just imagine!", That's how every game has to begin. It's the starting point for everything, the source of the magic that can transform a piece of wood into an ocean liner and gravel into gold. "Just imagine!", That is not only a gentle imperative to transcend the narrow confines of reality, but a wake-up call to the dormant powers of imagination. An archaic moment of play comes about when the most minimal of means mobilise a maximum of imagination and a simple object is all it takes to create a whole new world. In this sense, games are nothing less than a process of creation, in which the players are more or less playing God. In their hands, a simple object evolves into a universe which is peopled and shaped as the individual imagination sees fit.

That is what it must have been like for Friedrich Schleich when, at the end of the Second World War, he found himself faced with the meagre remains of his once flourishing factory for protective breathing devices. In a time of extreme hardship and privation, what was he supposed to do with his stores of wire and velvet? Perhaps we should picture Friedrich Schleich, in his mid-forties at the time, as a man gazing at a complete loss at these seemingly useless things, when he absentmindedly begins to bend the wire and fold the fabric and suddenly realises that what he's doing is playing. In fashioning the wire into a figurine and wrapping it in fabric, he transformed the leftovers of his disused factory into a toy whose most important component was not wire or velvet but imagination. The wire figurine that resulted from a bit of improvised playing marked an important turning point for the *Schleich* toy factory – the moment of its conception, as it were.

The past decade has seen the company return to those roots. The sensory experience of objects brought to life by an unspoilt imagination; the threefold combination of visual, tactile, and playful elements is intrinsic to *Schleich* products. With its renewed focus on a traditional, almost old-fashioned conception of play, the company is bucking the trend of increasing dematerialisation manifest in the non-tangible virtual games of the twenty-first century. These may represent an invitation into imaginary worlds of adventure and mind-blowing games, but the enchantment is restricted to the cold surface of a screen.

Man the player, homo ludens, was a creature of the Enlightenment. Poets and philosophers saw a playful approach to understanding the self and the world at large as the ideal path to what today we call self-fulfilment. In returning to the idealistic parameters of play, *Schleich* has returned to roots that are older than the company itself. In fact, they are as old as mankind.

The retrospective shows that the evolution of the company into its position today as an *Imaginative Play* world leader has not been a straight trajectory. But its confidence in its own potential and its return to a more traditional vision of play brought about its transformation, after the millennium, from a toy manufacturer heavily dependent on licensing and trends, into a strong brand with international recognition that in terms of ideas and development is entirely self-reliant. Today, *Schleich* products are widely known as toys that spark the imagination and are educational at the same time, conveying the riches of the natural environment to children as they play.

18

The success of the company's conceptual new departure marks a new chapter in its long and varied history – a history that reflects social and cultural change in its own particular way.

The growth of the company in the 1950s was inextricably tied to Germany's economic miracle. Schleich's hugely popular advertising mascots and characters not only represented the relaunch of the Gmünd-based company, they became symbols of the modern market economy that was fast gathering momentum. With the help of Schleich's advertising characters, shoe and watch manufacturers, petroleum and chemical companies, and tobacco firms gained popularity, customers, and a distinct image. With its designs, Schleich put a memorable face to these companies, but kept a low profile itself, restricting itself to its role as a supplier.

The dawning of the television era in the 1960s brought with it new marketing and advertising strategies that saw a drop in demand for advertising mascots and characters. New ideas were called for, and once again, the company managed to anticipate major technological and cultural changes, with a range of products adapted to suit new trends in consumer and entertainment culture. Schleich took the new cartoon characters out of the unattainable world of the TV screen and into children's playrooms, in the form of delightful, brightly coloured toy figurines. Today, the extraordinary, lasting popularity of characters such as Maya the Bee, Lucky Luke and, first and foremost, the Smurfs, seems unimaginable without the TV shows watched by all sectors of the population. But this undoubtedly successful business was dependent not only on the mass media, but also on costly licensing. The double dependency proved to be fatal when this market began to decline and the company's other lines of business were unable to compensate for it. The collapse came in the late 1980s, when the socially bonding function of TV family entertainment began to erode. New viewing habits, private stations as well as a general shift towards media pluralisation signalled the end for TV superstars such as Maya the Bee and the Smurfs. New characters, trends and fashions began to appear in rapid succession, minutely adapted to age and social class, for which television was little more than a media percolator. But Schleich rejected this fast-paced approach, choosing instead to return to its roots, focusing on marketing its traditional animal figurines, which in previous decades had been somewhat overshadowed by the successful cartoon characters. With its renewed emphasis on realistic farm and wild animal figurines, the company took an important step towards a market niche that distinguished it from other players and allowed it much greater scope for creativity and new ideas. The fact that the company turned its back on the volatile and costly licensing market was not a purely commercial move – it was also a decision in keeping with the company ethos. It was almost impossible to reconcile the company's high standards with the constant development and production of new series. Even today, most Schleich figurines are made by hand, and the creative process involved in the production of each toy miniature, be it a horse or a knight, is closely tied to the imaginative leap with which games begin. It always begins with an idea. This evolves into a design, a sketch or a drawing, which in turn serves as the blueprint for the modellers. Based in a small, almost cosy work-shop in an annex to the factory on the company's production site in Schwäbisch Gmünd, they spend weeks making something out of literally nothing. With the help of high-precision tools, they create a wax figurine, drop by drop. They refer to anatomical dictionaries and specialist tomes on zoology, experimenting, rejecting anything that doesn't work, ending up with an alabaster white, fragile-looking maquette on the table in front of them: the precursor to a new generation of Schleich figurines.

What comes next is a cloning process, which sees the wax figure joined by twins carefully hand-worked in silicone, ceramic, and metal – intermediary steps in the production of a casting mould which will be used in one of the 20 injection moulding machines on the factory floor. These heat and fluidify pigmented synthetic granules, which are then injected at high pressure (1600 bar) into the moulds. It is mostly women who work here; carefully they retrieve the finished, still warm figurines from the machines and soak them in cold water before placing them on chilled metal trays.

The artists work almost entirely without machines, painting the bare figurines to give them a realistic appearance. Decisions on how exactly the lionesses, penguin chicks, and domestic cats should ultimately look are made in the model painting department in Schwäbisch Gmünd. This is where two artists work, poring over the animal figurines and working out every nuance in fur colour and feathers with the help of photographs. A detailed blueprint is then passed on to large-scale workshops all over the world, where countless artists transform with a steady hand the raw moulds from Schwäbisch Gmünd into realistic reproductions of animals. These are then packed and sent back to the Schleich company warehouse, where they are kept until they begin their journey to children's playrooms all over the world.

Every Schleich figurine sold in toyshops has not only passed through many hands, it has also passed a series of strict tests. It is no accident that the department for quality control at the company headquarters in Schwäbisch Gmünd resembles a physics laboratory: In a number of special experimental plants, the figurines are put through a full check-up. The size of a tiger cub, for example, has to be monitored to ensure that it can't be swallowed by a three-year-old; a seal must not show sharp edges when someone bites on it, and even a large elephant has to be able to withstand hitting the ground when dropped from a great height before it can graduate to mass production. The background to these demanding tests are the many, internationally varied safety standards for children's toys, which have been tightened in recent years. Schleich products comply with the strictest standards laid down both in Europe and the United States.

The company's courageous decision to rely on its own creativity, entrepreneurial vision and, last but not least, experience, and to forge ahead with its original conception of play, appears to have captured the Zeitgeist. The sensory, tactile enjoyment of playing with figurines, the interaction from on high with a Lilliputian version of the world and the freedom to reorganise this world – none of this can be replaced by complex computer games or digital, virtual worlds. Today, Schleich figurines can be found in toyshops both large and small all over the world. Their understated authenticity sets them apart from the surfeit of cheap colour – there they are, waiting merely to be picked up, requiring neither an instruction manual nor a password. Just a little imagination. That's all.

Paul Kraut, Erich Schefold
Managing partners

Play is the source
of all that is good.
Friedrich Wilhelm August Fröbel

A tale of one man in his mid-forties, who turned to toys in troubled times and discovered that with a little imagination, even seemingly useless objects can be made magical – not just fun, but capable of reviving a factory's fortunes and helping him to keep a promise he had made to himself.

It's not as though the man sitting at his desk had never played with toys. But it had certainly been a while. And to a grown man and factory-owner, it felt very strange to be making a toy figurine. He fashioned the arms and legs from wire, a small head and feet from wood, and clothes from velvet. A toy was born. This man had spent decades successfully developing tools and technologies designed for protection against asbestos, carbon dust, and toxins, so what was he doing using the vestiges of this past to create a makeshift toy? Was this really the key to further success? In fact, all that was left to Friedrich Schleich, the man at the desk, of the factory that once made protective breathing devices, were a few rolls of velvet gathering dust in the storeroom, while the machines on the factory floor were still, and an oppressive sense of helplessness overshadowed the future of *Clora GmbH Schleich & Co.* The Second World War had just ended, the country was in ruins, and its people, paralysed with guilt and horror, were fearfully confronting a future that was uncertain, to say the least. Among them was Friedrich Schleich, who lived with his family in Schwäbisch Gmünd. It was here that he had founded his factory ten years previously. Now he faced the remnants of half his working life, a working life he had begun as a young, optimistic bank clerk. A combination of great talent, self-discipline, and ambition eventually led him to the top of a small company. His own company. So there he was, contemplating both the future and the past. And where it all began. Friedrich Schleich was born in 1900 to a penniless Bavarian couple who had moved to Swabia. He was taken in by a foster family even before he was christened. He grew up completely unaware

Industrial safety in the 1930s
By the time workers' health and safety came to be seen as an issue in Germany, rapid technological developments in mining, chemical engineering, and metallurgy had significantly raised the risk for people working in these industries. Adequate workwear and protective devices played an important role in increasing workplace safety.

Friedrich Schleich
No one could say that he was born with a silver spoon in his mouth, the boy who first saw the light of day in Feuerbach on 13 December 1900. The child of a very poor family, he grew up with foster parents. His early life was not an easy one, but he successfully made his way – a way which was to lead him to the top of his own company. After completing secondary school he became a bank clerk and at the age of 20 married his first wife, Hedwig, with whom he had two daughters. After a few years he resigned from the bank and worked as a freelance sales representative until, in 1926, the company Cloetta & Müller offered him a job. And that's how it all began.

of his true parentage, bearing the name of his foster parents and only learning of his background when he was confirmed. In a courageous move for someone so young, he then insisted on using his real name. His first foray into the world of work provided ample evidence that the self-assured young Friedrich Schleich could go far. He completed an apprenticeship with the prestigious Stuttgart bank Stahl & Federer and from 1922 to 1927 the public directory listed him as a bank clerk. But then, in the early years of the Weimar Republic, Friedrich Schleich resigned from the bank and began working as a freelance sales representative. Was it his undeniable free spirit that spurred him on, or perhaps other, extraneous factors? Whatever the immediate cause, he owed his success not only to his first-rate training and the resulting intimate familiarity with commercial matters, but also to his winning and persuasive manner. When Cloetta & Müller, a company founded in 1910 which specialised in industrial protective face masks, was looking to hire a sales representative, the company managers chose Friedrich Schleich. He began working for Cloetta & Müller on 1 January 1926. At the time he had been married for six years and was the father of a hopeful family. He soon proved indispensable to the company. As an enthusiastic sales rep, he not only tirelessly visited industrial companies, mines, and workshops, he also involved himself with technical developments which he hoped would optimise the efficiency of the protective masks. Despite his lack of any formal technical training, he managed to introduce real innovations as well as improvements. The new models developed by Friedrich Schleich allowed the company to avoid further frustrating disputes over patents with

Right
The company's first seat on Kronprinzenstraße, in Stuttgart

28

the Berlin-based rival company Auer, which in the past had involved Cloetta & Müller in legal proceedings over a number of products. In 1931 Friedrich Schleich registered the first utility patent in the area of industrial safety in his own name, followed by another 13 the following year. By now the company had been renamed Clora-Fabrikate Cloetta & Co. Atemschutzgeräte und Schutzbrillen to reflect its focus on breathing protection apparatus and protective goggles and was enjoying a stable turnover. In 1932 it began collaborating with the Auer factories on anti-gas defence. Clora ceded a number of proprietary rights to former rivals in this area and took over the sales of Auer products in southern Germany, abandoning its own production of protective masks against gas. In July 1933, its founder, Otto Cloetta, left the company. Friedrich Schleich was promoted manager and also acquired a holding in the company, now renamed Clora GmbH für Atemschutzgeräte. Times were tough. The Nazis had been in power since January 1933. Initially, Friedrich Schleich adapted to the new status quo, like most of his fellow countrymen. Even though he had never shown much interest in politics and saw himself first and foremost as a Swabian businessman, he joined the party. Presumably, he took this step in order to protect his business. Bearing in mind political developments in Germany at the time, it is perhaps not too hard to understand why a man who came from such humble beginnings would seek to protect at any price his hard-earned property with an opportunism founded on fear. But that is not to excuse it. Friedrich Schleich soon realised that not only Germany but the entire Continent was

The protective face masks were carefully handcrafted in the company workshops.

30

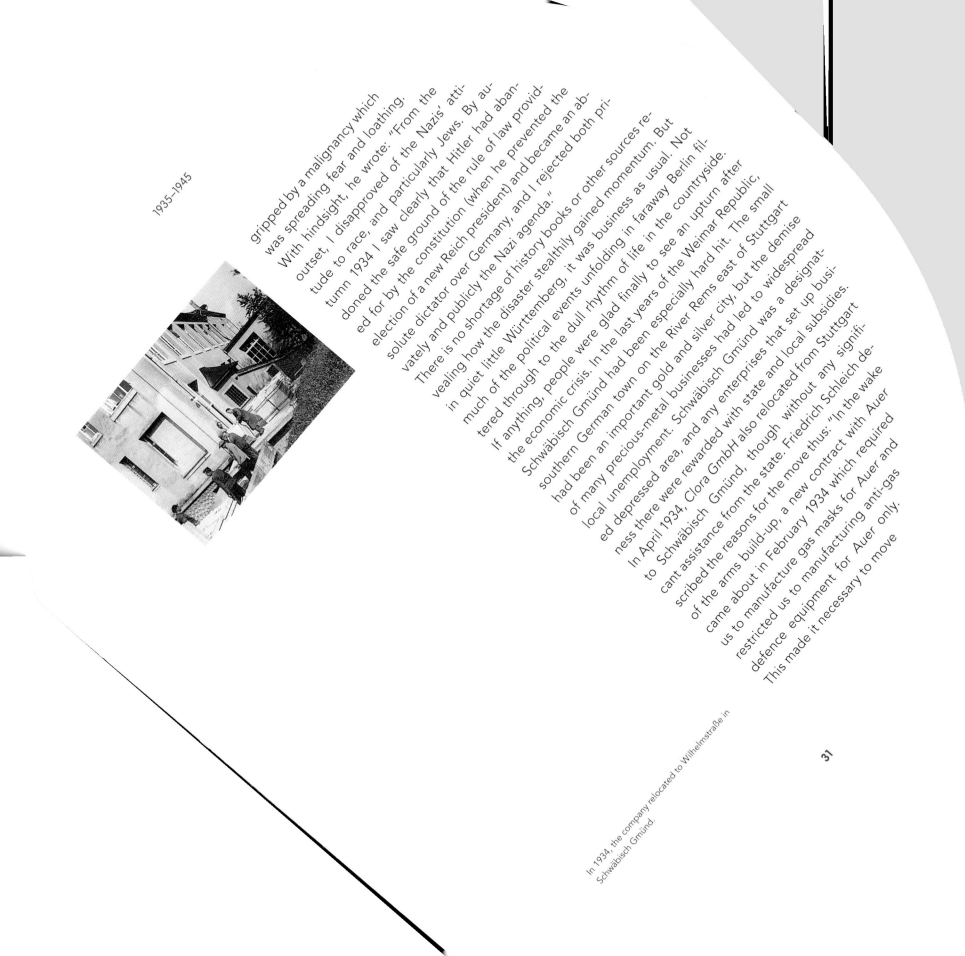

gripped by a malignancy which was spreading fear and loathing. With hindsight, he wrote: "From the outset, I disapproved of the Nazis' attitude to race, and particularly Jews. By autumn 1934 I saw clearly that Hitler had abandoned the safe ground of the rule of law provided for by the constitution (when he prevented the election of a new Reich president) and became an absolute dictator over Germany, and I rejected both privately and publicly the Nazi agenda."

There is no shortage of history books or other sources revealing how the disaster stealthily gained momentum. But in quiet little Württemberg, it was business as usual. Not much of the political events unfolding in faraway Berlin filtered through to the dull rhythm of life in the countryside. If anything, people were glad finally to see an upturn after the economic crisis. In the last years of the Weimar Republic, Schwäbisch Gmünd had been especially hard hit. The small southern German town on the River Rems east of Stuttgart had been an important gold and silver city, but the demise of many precious-metal businesses had led to widespread local unemployment. Schwäbisch Gmünd was a designated depressed area, and any enterprises that set up business there were rewarded with state and local subsidies.

In April 1934, Clora GmbH also relocated from Stuttgart to Schwäbisch Gmünd, though without any significant assistance from the state. Friedrich Schleich described the reasons for the move thus: "In the wake of the arms build-up, a new contract with Auer came about in February 1934 which required us to manufacture gas masks for Auer and restricted us to manufacturing anti-gas defence equipment for Auer only. This made it necessary to move

In 1934, the company relocated to Wilhelmstraße in Schwäbisch Gmünd.

production away from the danger zone."

War loomed on the horizon. Although Friedrich Schleich was not able to keep his business out of the general arms build-up, he continued to work tirelessly on the development of civilian protection equipment, intended for use in industry and mines, designing a steady flow of new models. He saw himself as an entrepreneur, dedicated to protecting the health of workers toiling at furnaces, in mines and chemical factories. On 18 September 1935, Friedrich Schleich appeared in the trade register as owner and sole manager of Clora Atemschutzgeräte Schleich & Co. Now it was official.

In the following years he was able to attract new investors. Three publishers from Stuttgart invested in Clora, allowing Friedrich Schleich to expand his business activities. He continued to concentrate on the flourishing business with protective masks for civilian use. By 1942 – well after the outbreak of war – he had registered a total of 60 patents and utility patents. He experimented with new materials, collaborated with professional associations pushing for binding standards on workers' health protection, and expanded his export business, which extended abroad through an international network of general agencies. But the successful business in protective equipment for workers was not enough to keep the company out of reach of the Nazi war machine, now firing on all cylinders. As with every business in Germany that was still operational, civilian production in Friedrich Schleich's company had to give way to the production of equipment needed for the war. Employees at the factory in Schwäbisch Gmünd worked double shifts producing protection masks for military use. Developing and

Above
The company's new premises in Stuttgart's Münster district opened in 1931.

Right
Entrance to the premises of the company Friedrich Schleich owned from 1935 on

32

manufacturing civilian products was soon out of the question. Despite continuous shortages of materials and staff and constant new regulations issued by the authorities, Friedrich Schleich did everything in his power to ensure his company and employees survived the war.

On 20 April 1945, when U. S. troops took Schwäbisch Gmünd, the local population put up no resistance. The end of the war marked the end of the Nazi regime. Even though his company was undamaged, Friedrich Schleich faced ruin. His entrepreneurial life was destroyed.

Like all industrialists whose businesses had continued manufacturing until the end of the war, Friedrich Schleich was arrested by the Allies and subjected to what was called a denazification programme. How much he blamed himself is revealed by a promise he made to himself: Were he ever to start another business, he told his staff, he would never again manufacture anything that could be used for purposes of war.

With that promise in mind, and as soon as permission came through, he rolled up his sleeves and began to rebuild his company. The Allies had confiscated everything required for the production of protective masks, leaving only the rolls of velvet that had been used to seal the masks.

Schleich sat at his desk, a roll of velvet in front of him. He had nothing else with which to start afresh. But in times of terrible hardship and penury, what good was velvet? It couldn't feed anyone; it was no good for rebuilding roads and houses. Velvet was useless, nothing but kid's stuff. At this thought, the man at the desk may have ventured a smile.

Clora GmbH presenting protective equipment for industrial workers at its trade fair stand

34

Top
Clora employed a large number of women,
mostly as seamstresses.

Bottom
Growing success also kept the accounting
department busy.

Playing is the children's path to knowledge of the world they live in!

Maxim Gorki

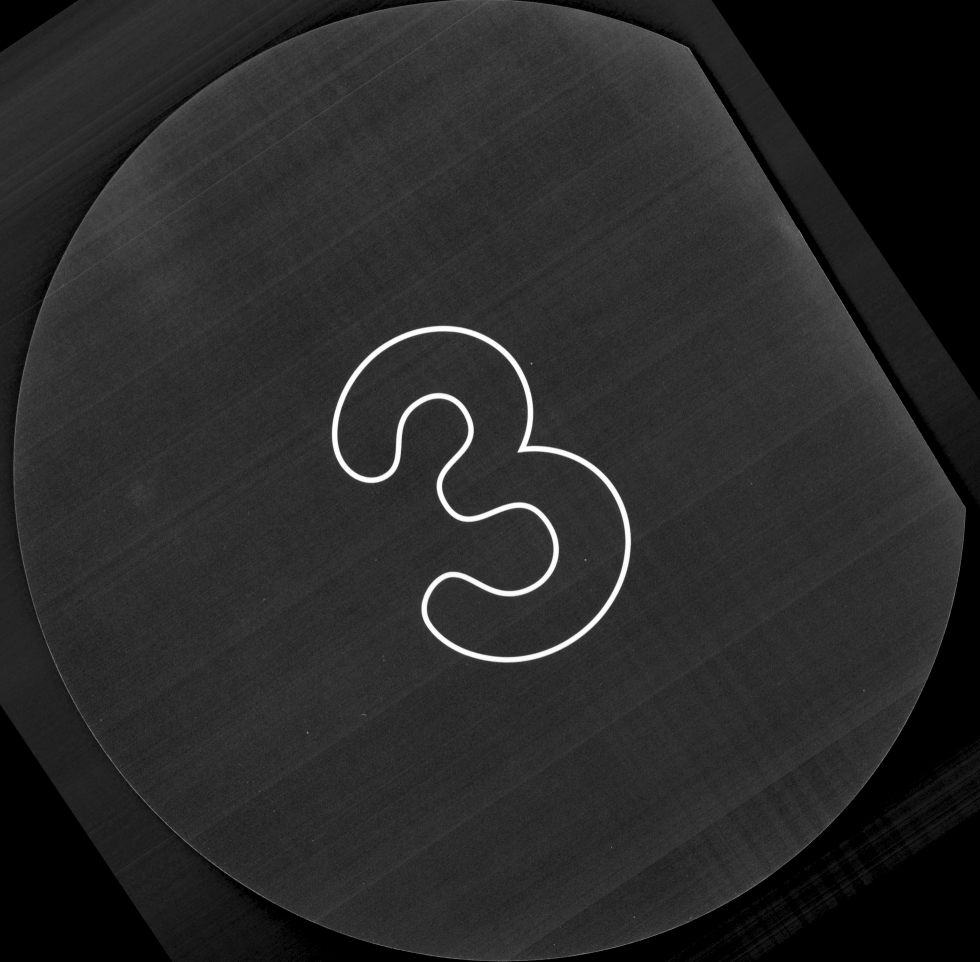

About a flexible black goblin with a soul of wire who founded a real dynasty, and later even received a memorial. And why a fire was started deliberately on the market square in Schwäbisch Gmünd, why an alien in London proved to be a false alarm, and why it was once suspected that Director Schleich had gone mad.

The plain wire doll clothed in velvet, joined in quick succession by other bendy figurines of the same construction, not only embodied a new start for Friedrich Schleich's business. In all its simplicity, it also exemplified the immediate postwar period as people improvised with left-overs, rejects, or completely unusable items, attempting to make something useful out of the little that remained to them.

Friedrich Schleich succeeded in obtaining the material needed for the manufacture of the wire dolls – wire, cloth, wood – and so supplied the seamstresses in his factory with work. Production started again. Bags, belts, briefcases, and even shoes were manufactured in addition to the dolls. For a time the product range included a baby carriage.

Spurred on by the success of the plain velvet doll, Friedrich Schleich began work on the development of a new toy figurine. He already had a fairly precise idea of its character and appearance. The new doll would be easily recognisable, robust, durable, and bendy; in short, a good sport. But the simple means used to date – wood, wire, and velvet – were not suitable for this ambitious innovation, which required both plastic and a completely new technology, namely, the pre-tensed wire procedure. This technique involved fitting three galvanised, tightly drawn wires – known as the wire soul – into an injection mould which was then filled with hot, liquid plastic. After cooling, the resulting body was removed from the mould and the ends of the wires, still under tension, cut off at the ends; and there it was, a slim, long-limbed doll, with bendy arms and legs as well as head and torso. The first seri-ally produced bendy toy from the Schleich company was a black

Advertising in the economic miracle years
Advertising in postwar Germany was rather a limited field. Posters and advertisements in newspapers or magazines were practically the only media in which to draw attention to a company or a product. Under these circumstances, companies hailed promotional figurines and mascots as an innovative possibility of generating customer loyalty and appeal as well as raising the rec-ognition factor of their brand.

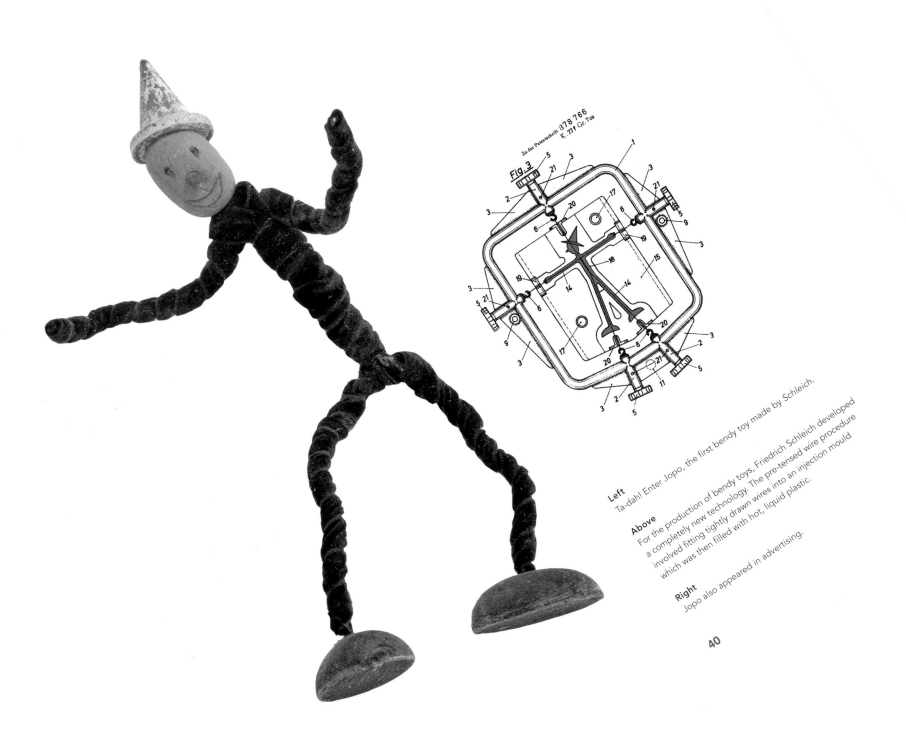

Left
Ta-dah! Enter Jopo, the first bendy toy made by Schleich.

Above
For the production of bendy toys, Friedrich Schleich developed a completely new technology. The pre-tensed wire procedure involved fitting tightly drawn wires into an injection mould which was then filled with hot, liquid plastic.

Right
Jopo also appeared in advertising.

40

goblin with a pointy nose and hat. Its name was Jopo. Its creator had drawn his inspiration from the eponymous picture book illustrated by a 20-year-old, up-and-coming art student at the Stuttgart State Academy of Art and Design, Eva Zippel.

Schleich's Jopo soon enjoyed great popularity. Production began at the start of 1946, and at the national trade fairs held shortly afterwards in Leipzig and Hanover, the company exhibited the toy figurine with great success. An exporter from Bremen even ordered 100,000 figurines for shipment to Great Britain. Jopo became a big seller – and a symbol of the dawn of a new age. In July 1946, Friedrich Schleich's company began trading under the name Clora Werkstätten Schleich & Co. In addition to toy production, the company also resumed the development and manufacture of industrial safety equipment and clothing. Thanks to the gradual increase in Germany's industrial production, the demand for modern health and safety protection was rising. And this was a field where Friedrich Schleich held numerous patents and technologies. A documentary on postwar industry in Schwäbisch Gmünd described operations at Clora Werkstätten: "From the very beginning, a laboratory for dust protection research, fitted with modern equipment, formed the starting point of production [...]. The decline of exports following the world war – which in the meantime have recovered to a gratifying extent – as well as changes in the production programme, forced the company to utilise the large sewing shop for other products. Thus protective clothing and special workwear [...] was included and developed in accordance with the special requirements of industry customers.

Eva Zippel, sculptor
Eva Zippel, born in Stuttgart in 1925, grew up in France, but later returned to her native city, where in 1946 she began to study sculpting at the Academy of Art and Design. It was around this time that Friedrich Schleich took notice of the aspiring artist. Eva Zippel began to work as a freelance modelmaker for the Gmünd-based toy company. Her designs shaped generations of toys from the first animal and toy figurines to the famous "advertising bendies". But she never gave up sculpting. During her years with Schleich she also created numerous sculptures, reliefs, and fountains. In 1975 she left Schleich and began to work for the city of Stuttgart, before eventually dedicating herself entirely to sculpting, which she pursued to a ripe old age.

Above
Friedrich Schleich (left) and Eva Zippel (right)

Right
A good sport: Jopo, the black goblin

Clora respiratory equipment (masks, filters, sponge rubber dust guards, sand blasting protection equipment, fresh air self-extractors, protective shields, etc.) is easily recognisable by its trademark, the word 'Clora' combined with a graphic symbol."

Throughout these years, Friedrich Schleich added numerous new developments to his already impressive portfolio of patents and proprietary rights in the field of industrial and respiratory protection. In addition to his products. Friedrich Schleich also knew how to draw spectacular attention to his products. In a long article from 15 May 1954, a local newspaper reported as follows: "A man was recently seen walking through the streets of London in an extremely unusual suit. Shocked passers-by stared at him as if he had come from another world. Even by the standards of a busy metropolis, the scene was more than bizarre: the man was clothed from head to foot in a glistening suit of armour. [...] 'Mister Tempex' from Schwäbisch Gmünd wasn't on his way to a film studio to feature in a science-fiction film about mysterious men from Mars, he was on his way to an industrial exhibition. [...] His protective clothing [...] enables him, despite intense heat, to stride into flames as if fire was a matter of no consequence. His suit shields him from the radiated heat in such a striking fashion that a temperature of – let us say – 2000 degrees has virtually no effect on him. Inside his protective clothing a thermometer indicates a temperature of 38 degrees centigrade. The Tempex Knight can pull the chestnuts out of the fire without getting burnt.

company now supplied thermal protective clothing, which was resistant to cold and wind as well as extreme heat. And

Top
Thermal protective clothing made in Schwäbisch Gmünd was resistant to cold and wind as well as extreme heat.

Bottom
Another Schleich product from the postwar years: Nefa baby carriages

44

And he has complete freedom of movement in his glittering garment, which is surprisingly light." The local public was also to be given an opportunity to witness the company's achievements. One afternoon a sizeable fire was lit on the market square in Schwäbisch Gmünd, and under the expectant gaze of onlookers a man swathed from head to foot in protective clothing strode into the middle of the leaping flames. He braved the heat long enough for the amazement of the bystanders to turn into blank horror. But as he emerged from the fire and removed the glittering silver suit there was hardly a drop of sweat on his brow – and the whole of Schwäbisch Gmünd now had a very lively idea of what was being manufactured "down at Schleich's". Even though the trade in protective clothing was more than satisfactory and the order books in Schwäbisch Gmünd were full, Friedrich Schleich decided to sell the division, including all patents and rights of sale. On 1 January 1957, it went to his former rival and collaborator in the area of industrial protection, the Berlin-based company Auer.

With this step, Schleich drew a line under the past. Even though it wasn't easy for him to say goodbye to his entrepreneurial roots, he was determined to put this troubled and troubling chapter in his history behind him. The promise that he had made to himself after the war played no small part in this. Thanks to the thriving career of Jopo, the bendy goblin, and the numerous siblings he had acquired in the course of time, the company was now able to concentrate on the expansion of its toy production. While only 13 figurines were available in 1950, the order form from 1957 listed more than 60 different

Top
"Don't be shy, come and look!"
A Jopo sales stand in the 1950s

Bottom
The sewing workshop also produced leather goods.

45

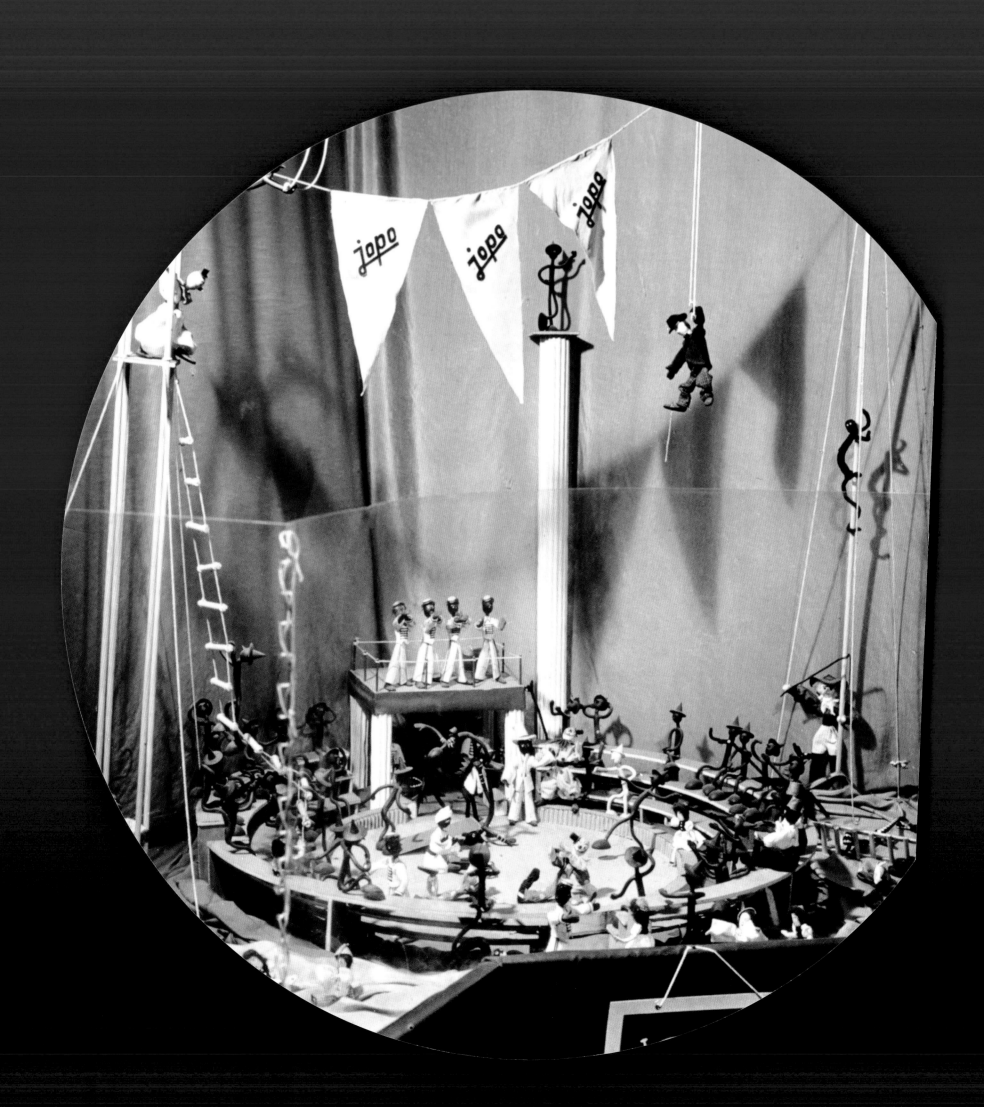

figurines: dolls, fairy-tale figures, animals, clowns, goblins. They all originated from the model workshop of the sculptor Eva Zippel, the former art student whose picture book had supplied the design for Jopo and who had modelled her first figurine for the Schleich company in 1946. Her successful debut was followed by countless other figurines which she continued to design for the toy factory in Schwäbisch Gmünd up until 1975. All this while the "Mother of Jopo" also worked as a freelance artist.

But Eva Zippel not only shaped whole generations of bendy toys, she also played a crucial role in the success of a completely new business line that opened up for the Schleich company in the mid-1950s: advertising mascots. Following the currency reform in 1948 and the founding of the Federal Republic of Germany the following year, an unprecedented period of dynamic economic growth began. The economic miracle saw an extraordinary increase in prosperity in which the whole of society shared. After the lean postwar decade, in which permits and rationing coupons shared up what little was available amongst the many who needed it, shop windows and shops were suddenly filled with all sorts of wares. New markets and products were competing for consumers who, thanks to the purchasing power of the Deutschmark, could now satisfy their wishes. In order to stand out amidst the abundance of a diverse, modern market, many companies employed the usual advertising measures to attract attention to their products and simultaneously win the loyalty of customers. Whether Lurchi from the shoe company Salamander, Aralbert from the Aral petrol stations, or the little Telefunken man – these

mascots transformed mass-produced utility goods into recognisable brand products, generating customer loyalty and appeal. Schleich manufactured these mascots, known as advertising bendies, at the behest of the respective companies, sometimes in large quantities. In 1961 the magazine Der Erfolg reported: "Bendy advertising mascots are 'customer models' which are not used for any other purpose, so that each mascot represents an individual model [...]. An advertising mascot can be used as a free gift, for decoration purposes, or as a bonus article [...]. These mascots can also be provided with advertising texts, for example in small booklets. The advertising mascot 'Aralbert' – the beaming petrol-pump attendant from BV-Aral – was handed out together with a humorous advertising booklet, 'The Girl of Good Breeding', comes with an advertising brochure about tic envelope. Similarly, the perky radiographer, 'The Girl of Good Breeding', comes with an advertising brochure about Structurix X-ray films from Gevaert [...]. A company that produces building protective agents [Hans Hauenschild] gave away the familiar tradesman types 'Hamburg carpenter' and 'Hamburg brick layer' in combination with promotional packs of matches, which also featured the two mascots."

The range of toy figurines also grew steadily. In addition to the plastic bendy dolls, 1955 saw the first foam rubber figurines, including the cartoon heroes Bambi and Pluto produced under licence from Walt Disney. In 1957 a series of non-bendable PVC animal miniatures was launched: a family of sea lions, an elephant, and a kangaroo, all modelled by Eva Zippel. His company's growing expertise in the field of plastics processing led Friedrich Schleich to consider expanding his product range. Thanks

Leggy, colourful, and cheery: plastic bendy toys

to rapid developments, above all in chemistry, the once expensive plastic could now be produced cheaply. And thanks to its in many respects more favourable characteristics, plastic had come to replace traditional materials such as metal, ceramic, textiles, or wood in a host of industries. Following the sale of the industrial protection division, Friedrich Schleich therefore turned to the growing demand for small plastic parts as he contemplated new strategies to supplement the ongoing toy production. In 1958 he renamed his company formplast Schleich & Co. to reflect this new focus on the development and manufacture of plastic components. An article in the industry magazine einhorn stated in 1963:

"The main focus of the production programme is in the technical sector, the processing of a wide range of plastics, some of them developed in-house, for the production of industrial mouldings. The joint work of laboratory, engineering department, and mould construction, managed by seasoned specialists, allows solving even the most complicated problems. As a result, increasing numbers of accessory parts, previously made of metal, are now manufactured from the much more suitable plastic. Apart from important foreign companies, a number of Gmünd-based enterprises have also consulted the Formplast company: they, too, are now able to process better and cheaper components."

Due to the company's rapid growth, space in the head office, housed in a period building in Gmünd's Wilhelmstraße, was beginning to be somewhat cramped. As there were no expansion possibilities in the neighbourhood, the search was on for a new location. A suitable plot of land was found in Herlikofen, a village that was later incorporated

Advertising leaflet and lettering designs from the 1950s

49

Above
All-American Cowboy: Lucky Luke

Right
Bendies designed by Eva Zippel

CLOWN

1946–1964

MORITZ

HOTTO

PIPS

MAX

51 BOY

KAMEL

Left
Bendy bad boys: Max and Moritz plastic toys

Above
Sketches and drawings for new bendy dolls

53

into Schwäbisch Gmünd, and during the course of the purchase Friedrich Schleich also secured an option on the adjacent land. The building work for the new factory began in September 1958, and as early as July the following year the production of plastic parts was transferred to the new premises. The production of toy figurines and advertising mascots began a few months later. Step by step, the administration departments were also transferred from Schwäbisch Gmünd to Herlikofen, and with the completion of a second production hall and the opening of the model painting department in March 1963, the relocation of the company to its new address, Am Limes 69 in Herlikofen, was finally completed.

At that time the company employed nearly 100 workers, as well as providing work for over 200 female homeworkers in the local area. Friedrich Schleich and his family also moved to Herlikofen, where he had a house built close to the factory, together with stables for his riding horses. An entrepreneur of the old school, greatly concerned with social prestige, he played an active role at the site of his new factory, supporting the village associations with generous donations. The majority of his employees came from Herlikofen; the new company was the largest employer in the locality. Thanks to his natural authority and friendly manner, he won the respect of both local dignitaries and workers, cultivating the dependable routines that bolstered his reputation as a respectable businessman. Few people were aware that he also had an eccentric, adventurous streak. Thus, one Shrove Tuesday, Herlikofen was astonished to see the sophisticated gentleman riding through the village to his factory, dressed in a colourful costume. Mounted on his

Top
The saw-tooth roof clearly shows that this building taking shape at the company's new location in Herlikofen is a factory.

Bottom
The company's new site with the Swabian Alb in the background. It was situated near the Rhaetian Limes bounding the ancient Roman provinces.

horse, he knocked on the windows behind which the more than dumbfounded workers were seated, and, without further ado, proclaimed that the factory was closed for the afternoon. Then he rode away again. At *Schleich* people shook their heads. Had the boss gone mad? Friedrich Schleich was hard to fathom. What lay behind the serious façade of the respectable businessman remained hidden even from the people closest to him. Many knew, however, that the question of his succession plagued him very much, an issue that remained unresolved for a long time. As his two daughters showed little interest in the fortunes of the company, he placed all his hopes in his son-in-law Volkmar Klaus, who he systematically groomed as a future company director. The company founder was very concerned to see his life's work pass into the hands of a family member; for Friedrich Schleich, as has already been said, was a factory owner of the old school.

Top
Production of plastic bendy toys. Note the frame with the pre-tensed wires the worker is holding in her hands.

Bottom
It was no secret that Friedrich Schleich had a penchant for horses.

Left Some bendies came dressed in elaborate costumes handmade by homeworkers in and around Schwäbisch Gmünd.

Above Schleich's bendies populated a whole universe of toys.

Right The grimacing finger-masks of soft plastic were meant for fun rather than play.

Below
Advertising mascots made by *Schleich*

Right
Schleich trade fair stand, with company owner Friedrich Schleich in the middle

People do not stop playing
because they grow old; they grow old
because they stop playing.

Oliver Wendell Holmes

A bribery attempt with French pâté; how Smurfs suddenly outnumbered residents in Schwäbisch Gmünd; and what brought Herr Schneider and five Chinese visitors to Frau Straube's for cake and coffee.

The company in Herlikofen received in 1965 an order from the petrol firm BP for small, blue plastic figurines that BP was planning to give away as free promotional gifts. The blue-skinned dwarfs were characters from the popular Johan and Peewit stories created by the Belgian cartoonist Peyo. The "Schloumpfes", as they were called in the cartoon strips, played only a relatively small role in Peyo's stories. But the amusing characters with comical pointy caps, childlike round faces, large eyes and knobbly noses, seemed appropriate as cheery promotional figures. Schleich made large numbers of the blue dwarfs, and at first the company regarded this as just another commission. The enormous popularity of the figurines took both BP and Schleich by surprise, but soon the manufacturers were thinking of the next logical step: professional marketing and merchandising of the Schloumpfes.

The first television appearance came in 1968, when the German network ZDF created a TV series starring the Schloumpfes. Many German households did not yet own a television set at the time, so the series did not quite succeed in creating a large market, but Schleich continued to manufacture the blue dwarfs. They were renamed "Schlümpfe" or "Smurfs" in 1972, and until 1973, the company catalogue featured a string of new Smurf characters, and even a Smurf house.

But from 1975 on, Schleich stopped manufacturing the figurines. This had less to do with their modest economic success than with developments behind the scenes. Friedrich Schleich's designated successor, his son-in-law Volkmar Klaus, had left the company after a family row. Rumour had it that there were differences between him and

Children's television from the 1960s The age of television had its own heroes. During the 1960s, television emerged as a broad-based medium that gradually replaced the previously ubiquitous radio. Initially, TV sets were expensive status symbols, but from the mid-1970s at the latest almost every family had one. As television began to reach wider audiences, programmes were designed to attract particular viewer groups, including children. The success of cartoon characters like Maya the Bee, Lucky Luke, or the Muppets would not have been possible had it not been for children's programmes and the millions of little viewers that watched them.

Left
Ready to take over children's toy boxes all over the world: the Smurfs

Top
The successor and his wife: Hermann Schneider took over as managing director in 1976.

Bottom
Sculptor Eva Zippel and Friedrich Schleich. Together they shaped generations of toys.

Schleich's second wife who, unlike the first wife, Hedwig, refused to be satisfied with the purely representative role of a spouse and insisted on having a voice in company decisions. Volkmar Klaus brought the long-standing rivalries to an end by walking out on the firm in 1973 and founding a competing toy company, *Bully*, in nearby Spraitbach. The initial success of *Bully* can be attributed to two factors: first, the handful of experienced workers who followed Klaus from *Schleich* and, second, the rights to the manufacture of the Smurfs, which Klaus successfully wrested from his father-in-law. From this point on, *Schleich* had no rights to produce or distribute the blue dwarfs.

For Friedrich Schleich, now over 70 years old, both were painful losses. More than ever before, he needed a successor to take over the reins of the firm, and, almost overnight, he had lost a successful product in which he had invested a great deal of time and money.

In 1975, by the time of the company's 40th anniversary and his 75th birthday, Schleich was looking more confidently towards the future. At a conference of the professional association for toy manufacturers, he had met Hermann Schneider, an extraordinarily talented and multilingual businessman from the Black Forest region, who had previously worked for the American greeting card company *Hallmark*. In Schneider, now the manager of a playing card company, Schleich found a man after his own heart, who from humble beginnings had made a remarkable career for himself through hard work, good luck, and sheer talent. Schneider was not only a good partner to have in one's business but also, Schleich believed, someone to whom he could bequeath his life's work, the product of 40 years of industriousness.

On 1 January 1976, Hermann Schneider took over as the second managing director of the company, partnering with Friedrich Schleich. A year later, Schleich sold his share of the company and went into well-deserved retirement. Hermann Schneider now became the owner and senior managing director of the company, and he named Giovanni Trimboli, a business associate of long standing, as his assistant director. There was a fresh wind blowing in Herlikofen, and it wasn't coming from the Swabian Alb. Hermann Schneider saw that he had taken over a company that was beginning to show its age. Profits had been declining for some time, and the company had done nothing to counter that trend. Too long had it depended on past successes. Potential for new forms of marketing and product innovation had been left untapped. Hermann Schneider decided to renovate. First, he gave the company image a new look. The logo he launched is still the existing one: a bold red "S" inside a circle. The idea was to give the long-established toy manufacturing company a new face and to make the logo a classic that would stand the test of time, as indeed it has. Then, Schneider invested in merchandised products made famous by radio and television. The first product line under his aegis included not only the Muppets, the Peanuts gang, and the Sandman, but also the Smurfs. After tough legal battles with the rival company *Bully*, Schneider had won back the rights for producing the blue dwarfs. The international licences for the characters, now famous through comics and children's film series, were expensive but proved to be worth the cost.

1957–1977

1957–1962

1961–1962

1961–1963

1963–1977

from 1978

Logo

It's in their feet. If you want to know to which generation a *Schleich* figurine belongs, you have to look at their feet, or rather, at the mark that all figurines made by *Schleich* bear on the soles of their feet. This mark will enable you to determine with some precision when a bendy toy or animal miniature was made. Up until 1961, all figurines were marked with a vertical box with the lettering "Schleich's Biegefiguren" around the top and bottom inside edge. The next development was for the box to turn into a circle, and in 1963 the circle was given a tapering bold edge and the lettering was reduced to the simple "Schleich". The year 1978 saw the introduction of the logo that is still used for all *Schleich* figurines today, the famous "S" in a circle. Apart from these widely-used logos, there are some that are extremely rare. The figurines that bear them have turned into collector's items; they mostly hail from the early 1960s and mark non-bendable figurines.

Television had played an increasingly important role for the company, even in the last years under Friedrich Schleich. One of the company's greatest successes in the first half of the 1970s were the "Wum and Wendelin" figurines, a dog and elephant duo created by the humorist Loriot and made famous by ZDF. Soon after merchandising began in 1973, the company made a donation agreement whereby 40 pfennigs from the sale of each figurine (sold at 2 Deutschmarks) would be donated to ZDF's Aktion Sorgenkind, a campaign which raised money for children with disabilities. The figurines and the donation campaign were given air time on a prime-time television show, and the following day, a motorcade of vehicles could be seen streaming into the little town of Herlikofen. People who had been inquiring after the Loriot figures in toyshops everywhere had been directed to Schleich in Herlikofen. By 1985, Schleich's Wum and Wendelin figures had pulled in 4,325,751.95 Deutschmarks for the Aktion Sorgenkind campaign.

Under the leadership of Hermann Schneider the firm had, for the first time in its history, recognised and systematically mined the economic opportunity afforded by the firmly entrenched culture of television. In a strategic move, Schneider now set his sights on licensing and internationalisation, harnessing the power of mass-media pop culture to drive business in Herlikofen. Looking back, we can say that the phenomenon of the Smurfs is the best-known example worldwide of a product that became a sure-fire success because of radio and television. In 1983, 25 years after they came into being, the Smurfs were hailed by the Wall Street Journal as the "Toy of the Year"; they were

Top and middle
Television history made tangible: Wum and Wendelin

Bottom
Vucko was the official mascot of the 1984 Winter Olympics held in Sarajevo; Schleich's figurines depicted all disciplines represented at the games.

the subject of thoughtful reviews in feature pages; and Hermann Schneider himself found it difficult to account for this extraordinary success: "Our performance is atypical in the current economy; we are bucking the trend where markets demand streamlining." He knew what he was talking about. In Herlikofen, production could no longer keep up with demand for the blue dwarfs. Worldwide demand had completely outstripped all projections. One morning, a retailer from the Alsace region suddenly appeared with his truck in front of the factory entrance. He could no longer persuade his disappointed customers to wait for the next scheduled delivery of Smurfs and vowed that he would not return without a large stock of the figurines. To shore up his verbal pleas, he presented bewildered Schleich employees with a large packet of delicious French pâté.

At this point, the firm was producing more than 250 different Smurf characters in various locations in South America, Europe, and Asia, which were then distributed to destinations around the world from headquarters in Herlikofen. The little Swabian village, with its half-timbered houses and tidy beds of primroses, had become the capital of international toys. Tucked away up in the Swabian Alb, it was hardly prepared for this role. One Sunday, Hermann Schneider, who was hosting a five-person delegation visiting from China, realised that there was no restaurant to which he could take his guests. Nothing daunted, he decided to knock on the door of Heidemarie Straube, an employee in the sales department, and asked if she could offer his guests homemade cake and coffee. Frau Straube could indeed offer both and warmly welcomed the

Left
Welcome to the Smurf village!

Top
Toy of the Year 1983: Smurfs from
Schwäbisch Gmünd

Bottom
A world of its own: the Smurf universe

group into her home. Thus five Chinese visitors and a delighted managing director signed business agreements while sitting around Frau Straube's coffee table, and the Asian visitors probably returned home with a rather curious idea of German family-run businesses. These were extraordinary times in Herlikofen.

The company was working beyond its limits. Production as well as storage capacity was exhausted. Large packages with millions of Smurfs, ready for delivery, had to be temporarily stored in makeshift beer tents to protect them from wind and weather. In 1984, to keep up with the seemingly infinite boom, construction began of a high-rise warehouse in extension to the company site. While business was concentrated on the production and marketing of Smurfs, the company continued obtaining licences for comic or TV figures, extending its series of miniature animals with small and large versions, and producing the carnival emblems with local motifs that were so popular in the region.

To prevent becoming too dependent on the marketing success of the licensed figures, the company decided to introduce a brand new product in 1982: project S-Point. The new educational series consisted of nine colourful construction kits for children to build various vehicles. The additional investment for new machines, moulds, and tools ran into several million Deutschmarks, and the new product was displayed at the Nuremberg Toy Fair with much optimism. But success was elusive. Were the construction kits too complicated, too expensive, or just unequal to the competition? Nobody at Schleich had a clue. No one there anticipated the consequences of the failure of S-Point.

Left
A model car from the S-Point series

Top
Pride and optimism: Hermann Schneider at the 1985 Toy Fair

Bottom
For many years the product range included a board game with bendy pegs invented by Friedrich Schleich.

Below
Maya the Bee, Willi, Flip, and Thekla the Spider
with their friends

Right
It's time to meet the Muppets!

72

Above
The Ottiphants are the trademark of
German comedian Otto Waalkes.

Right
Good Ol' Charlie Brown and the rest
of the Peanuts gang

The true sign of intelligence
is not knowledge but imagination.

Albert Einstein

The toughest day of Herr Mehner's working life and why Herlikofen was long under a cloud of oppressive uncertainty. How Herr Brauer came to be the best-dressed lorry driver in Baden-Württemberg and even the Smurfs found their destiny changed by world history.

And then everything seemed to happen at once. While the investments poured into expansion and the new product left the company reeling, the S-Point series proved once and for all to have been a costly mistake. As if that were not dramatic enough, demand for the Smurfs fell more or less overnight. The market was saturated. Over 25 million unwanted Smurfs sat on the shelves in Herlikofen. Business with the other figurines was still reasonable, but yielded nowhere near enough to cover the company's expensive commitments, let alone the acquisition of further licences or investment in the development of new products. In 1986, the balance sheets were disastrous, and the outlook was bleak. By January 1987, the company had to declare itself bankrupt. No one had any idea what the future held.

The question was simple. What could be done with the company? Was there any potential for a new beginning? And if so, what kind of new beginning? Hermann Schneider, the company's talented, infectiously enthusiastic and persuasive owner and manager, had managed to steer the company to its considerable success, but now he faced complete ruin. Since he had charged all his own assets, he ended up heavily in debt. He too had run out of ideas.

Among the many unanswered questions, one thing was clear: rescuing the company would require some tough measures. Not only were staff keen to see a rescue – suppliers and former business partners also wanted the company to survive, and not just for sentimental reasons. Along with the Scholz company based in the nearby town of Essingen, Franz-Ulrich Köster, Klaus K. Schwarz, and Paul Kraut Senior got on board as new partners. While Paul

Child's play: digital media
In the 1980s, rapid growth in the toy market and a wide range of highly diversified and often short-lived radio and television programmes for children undermined the bonding function that some of these characters and stories had had. The entrance of digital media into the world of children accelerated this process: fun and games were no longer sought in the toy box but on the screen. The educational value of these entertainments is often questionable.

79

Kraut Sr. was already a close associate of the company, new shareholders Franz-Ulrich Köster and Klaus K. Schwarz were two long-standing employees. As majority shareholder, Scholz appointed Heinz Kurt Wahren as CEO. Insolvency administrator Rüdiger Mocker drew up a strategy which involved the division of the company into two independent enterprises, Schleich-Produktions-GmbH and Schleich-Spielzeug-Vertriebs-GmbH. These dramatic measures also necessitated staff cutbacks. Factory manager Heinz Mehner, who had worked for the company for more than twenty years, ensuring that everything ran smoothly on the factory floor, was given the dreaded task of firing 50 percent of each department. A man of integrity and compassion, he knew every single one of the company's 69 employees, some of them for many years. He knew their families, their life stories, and their troubles. And now he had to decide who could stay and who had to go.

When he was finished with his list, Mehner despaired. A man of integrity and compassion, he passed it on to Heinz-Kurt Wahren, one of the new CEOs, who broke the terrible news at a staff meeting. Given that Schleich was the main employer in the region, and that members of just about every family in Herlikofen had once worked for the company as an employee or homeworker, the funereal mood in the factory and on the streets was inevitable. Even though the new investors still hoped to turn around the ailing company's fortunes, and the local authorities, banks, and employment exchange cushioned the blow of the austerity measures first and foremost for the company's sacked employees, the pinch was still felt in the day-to-day running of the business. If anything needed to be

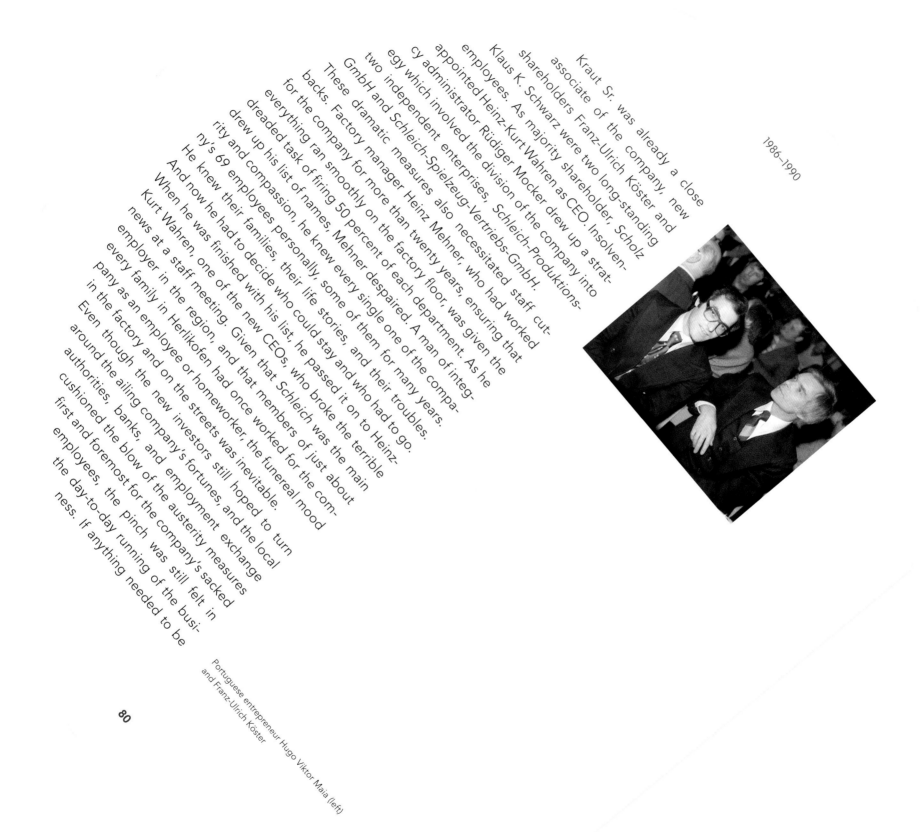

Portuguese entrepreneur Hugo Viktor Maia (left) and Franz-Ulrich Köster

serviced or repaired, the employees had to bring their own tools from home, because the company lacked the money for new equipment. The workers who hadn't been laid off, but had to make do with short-term contracts, did their best. But the machines were often turned off for days on end, and a ghostly quiet descended on the factory grounds.

Behind the scenes, management was feverishly searching for strategies to secure the company's long-term future. It could count on its fine reputation as a professional toy manufacturer. However, it not only lacked the funds for new, ambitious licensing acquisitions that would enable it to develop and market cartoon characters, everyone agreed that the company should no longer be so reliant on short-term and expensive licensing deals that depended on the whims of easily bored and unpredictable TV viewers. At the Haghof, a remote golf club in the Swabian Forest near Stuttgart, the new management and departmental heads held crisis talks that would later become legendary, deciding on a drastic plan to boost the profitable, more robust parts of the business. It was obvious that the loss-making units would have to go.

For lack of a fundamentally new strategy for the toy unit, management concentrated on a radical reduction of the Smurf range and attempted to gain a footing in the giftware market. Advertising mascots played as little a role in the company's future plans. But another company classic, miniature animal figurines, remained part of the scaled-back catalogue. In this difficult year, these basic, realistic little model animals provided the comfort of

Catalogues from 1988 to 1990

old friends. As well as a revamp of the toy unit, the new owners' overhaul plans included an expansion of the industrial plastics processing division. To this end, Schleich-Kunststofftechnik GmbH was founded in 1988 to manufacture small parts and components in its injection moulding machines. Henceforth, parts manufactured by Schleich were to be found in everything from Märklin train sets to Gardena garden tools, Carl Zeiss Oberkochen optical instruments, Hilti heavy equipment, and Triumph underwear fasteners. The rapid success of this part of the business was due entirely to the staff's pioneering spirit and commitment. Despite the increase in orders, the company was still operating pretty much hand-to-mouth, so employees often had to load boxes of small parts into the back of their own cars and deliver them in person. Wolfgang Brauer, a young man who had recently returned to Germany from the United States to look after technical procedures at Schleich's, had a habit of combining a few deliveries with his frequent meetings with business customers' technical departments. So he was often to be seen behind the wheel of a lorry in a suit and tie: first he would drive to the delivery entrance with the goods, then he would head off with his plans and technical designs for discussions on the executive floor.

After months of agony, a new mood of optimism reigned in Herlikofen – at least among the employees of the plastics processing division. Over in toys, they were still searching for a viable way forward. Even though people the world over had happy associations with the name "Schleich" – "Oh, yes, the Smurfs", they would nod – the company was still in trouble. At toy and games fairs, the modest

Left
All creatures great and small: European wildlife en miniature

Above
Dinosaurs appeared as early in the product range as they did in Earth's history.

giftware and joke items on display at the Schleich stands were barely a dull echo of the golden era of the Smurfs. The novelties went as fast as they came.

Looking back, no one can quite remember who came up with the idea that ultimately saved the company. And to be precise, there were actually several ideas – simple and practicable and as such, wholly in keeping with the old-established Schleich company tradition. Basically, the idea consisted of a return to the company's original concept: the plain, nameless figurine with which it all began. Instead of investing in costly licences for figures and characters from comics and TV series, the company decided to concentrate on producing and marketing its own designs – realistic, miniature animals created, made, and hand-painted by the company itself. The company had learned its lesson from the abrupt end of the Smurf boom in the mid-1980s and its unfortunate consequences. The fact that this insight was followed up with the necessary steps was largely the work of CEO Franz-Ulrich Köster and Klaus Weißhaar, then the company's head of marketing. They were the ones who pushed for a renaissance of Schleich's traditional toy. By turning its back on licences and returning to its roots, the company gained new self-confidence in one great swoop. And it seemed fitting that the fundamental transformation taking place in Herlikofen occurred at a time when the whole world was beginning to change: in 1989.

The end of the Cold War, German reunification in 1990, and the opening up of Eastern Europe, paved the way for the Smurfs' great comeback. In those countries, the little blue creatures had been familiar for years, but had never been on sale. What then happened was what economists call "catch-up consumerism" – now that they could, people started buying everything they'd ever coveted. And this included Smurfs from Herlikofen, who still had a place in the Schleich catalogue, even if the range had been scaled back in terms of breadth and variety. The Smurfs' unexpected second wind marked a triumphant end to a great, significant, and wonderful era, and simultaneously the start of a new one.

The stuff that toys are made of
If some figurines are malleable and soft to the touch while others feel solid and robust, that is because they are made of different materials. The production of Schleich toys involves up to ten different types of plastic, each chosen for its perfect suitability for the toy in question. Moreover, Schleich is committed to research in new materials known as biopolymers. This new, biodegradable type of plastic is remarkable for its sustainability, too.

Happiness is not an ideal of reason but an ideal of imagination.

Immanuel Kant

6

How it came about that all animals are tagged at the leg, why some polar bears come from North Africa and why Swabian dinosaurs arouse scientific interest in Berlin and elsewhere. And finally, a peek at new developments behind the scenes.

When the management decided to establish the company as a specialist, top-end manufacturer of realistic miniature animals, they were not just correcting the course. Schleich had a tradition of producing model animals, which had been a fixed part of the company's repertoire since the 1960s. So while, on the one hand, this step ensured continuity, on the other, it was a chance to start systematically reinventing the company. No other firm besides Schleich produced animal figurines with such care and attention to detail. Every single model, whether a lion cub or an Asian cow elephant, had to be approved by experts from the Berlin Zoo before it went into production. They checked each prototype to make sure that it was anatomically correct, advised about colouring, and provided information about the species' behaviour, habitat, and other interesting facts.

The shift away from the more stylised animal figurines based on designs by Eva Zippel had already begun in the mid-1970s when the modelmaker Werner Joos took over from the Stuttgart sculptor. Though he did brilliant work on the Smurfs, Joos really favoured realistic imitation, as is evident in those Schleich series which from 1986 onwards came to define the company's product range. All those animals big and small, today's classics, sprang from his creative hands.

It was not only the new product strategy that helped make the company's reinvention a success. Schleich was singularly fortunate in its partners and suppliers at home and abroad. The fresh start would not have been possible without the trust of the people at Maia, a family business based in Portugal, or of C. Y. Lee, the company's former

The online revolution The internet has not only revolutionised the way we communicate, but also the way we play. Children of all ages are today confronted with a bewildering range of virtual games whose imaginative design and attractive graphics may kindle the imagination to fantastic fireworks. At the same time, these games deprive children of the wonderful experience of actually doing things, taking things in their hands, and inventing new worlds of their own.

office manager in Hong Kong, whom the bankruptcy forced to establish his own business, or of Kraut, a family-owned business based in Burghaslach, in Bavaria. Of course, more immediately tangible factors also played a role. Schleich's animal figures were so outstanding in quality not least because the company had continually upgraded the technology used in its industrial plastics processing division. The technical innovation that had taken place over a number of years now substantially benefited toy production, too. Probably the most important sign to the outside world, however, was a small, white tag with the company logo. Attached to the foot of each figure, it made every single one a clearly branded product. This simple measure gave the miniature animals a well-deserved aura of exclusiveness, identifying them as unique pieces with a substantial handcrafted element. At the same time, a new concept was being developed for their presentation in toyshops and department stores. No longer would assorted animal figures be put on sale in rummage bins or simply placed in cardboard boxes, as if they were two a penny. Instead, they would be put on show in specially designed, high-class displays.

In the early 1990s the company began to collaborate with the U. S. manufacturer Safari on a number of series; these included the Carnegie Collection with miniature dinosaurs, a collection of marine animals, as well as two groups with wild animals and animal families. Schleich responded to the dinomania unleashed by the film Jurassic Park in 1993 with its own eight-piece dinosaur collection. For the first time in its history it also offered soft toy versions, child-sized battery-driven models, and stylised cartoon

True to life and hand-painted: a beautiful grey from the horse product line

dinosaurs, though here it was merely acting as a distribution partner for an Asian manufacturer. While the soft toys, the mechanical monsters, and their comic cousins were discontinued once the stock was sold, the realistic replicas remained in the product range. The dinosaur figures were created in cooperation with Professor Böhm, a palaeontologist at the Museum of Natural History in Berlin, who scrutinised all dinosaur models presented by Schleich according to strict scientific criteria. As a result, Schleich dinosaurs were not only used as toys, they also made an appearance in biology lessons, in dioramas of primordial times, and in natural history exhibitions about the flora and fauna of the Jurassic Age.

The company's own successful creations now dominated Schleich's catalogue of goods for sale; in fact, for all, those comic figures that had previously loomed so large. While in the 1990s there were a number of new runs of such well-known cartoon figures as Maya the Bee, the Peanuts gang, and the heroes of the popular German children's series known abroad as Mouse TV, they never made a real breakthrough, nor did the tentative attempts to relaunch bendy toys or advertising mascots come to fruition. Over the years, they disappeared from the company's product range and entered the somewhat curious parallel world of collectors and enthusiasts' catalogues.

By the mid-1990s at the very latest, Schleich was an established toy manufacturer. For its international expansion plans the company was able to rely on a closely-knit distribution network dating back to the Smurf era, which extended overseas and as far as the Asia-Pacific area. In

Left and above
The wide World of History is populated by primordial beasts like Giganotosaurus.

addition to the manufacturing plant in Herlikofen, capacity was expanded in China, Portugal, and Tunisia. Every single figure is still individually hand-painted in one of these places before being sent back to Germany ready for distribution. And this is why all of Schleich's polar bears have been to North Africa, and why a German brown hare might have first seen the light of day in the Far East. Some other equally decisive changes were taking place behind the scenes of the successful relaunch. The firms set up in 1995 to form the *Schleich Produktions- und Handelsgesellschaft mbH*, an umbrella organisation, were merged in 1987 for both the toy and the plastics section, which still actually closed in the year 2000. In 1997 the shares owned by the Scholz company were acquired by the remaining partners Köster, Kraut, and Schwarz. Things were looking up.

Paul Kraut Junior, son of co-partner Paul Kraut Senior, joined Schleich in Herlikofen in 1999. The graduate engineer and qualified businessman had known the company from an early age, for as a small boy he had often helped out in his father's firm. It was responsible for the delivery of the figures, which, at that time, were still being painted at home by cottage industry workers. He had practically grown up with the company in Herlikofen. Initially, Paul Kraut Jr. worked in production planning, but within a short space of time he was also entrusted with management responsibilities both at the company headquarters and at its production sites in China and Tunisia. As chief executive officer, Franz-Ulrich Köster saw it as his job to ensure the future of the company. Rather than regarding the

Left and above
In the World of Fantasy, the dragon lies down with the unicorn and the elf.

young, talented engineer as a natural heir to the company throne because he was the son of a co-partner, he judged him to be a suitable successor on his own merit. As Franz-Ulrich Köster stepped down in 2003, he could rest assured that Schleich was in good hands. Admittedly, Paul Kraut Jr., who has headed the company since 2004, did not have much time for the patriarchal aspects of the company's structure. And so he seized the opportunity that presented itself when the old partners Köster, Schwarz, and Kraut Sr. sold their shares to the British private equity fund HG Capital in 2006. The new majority stakeholder represented a strong partner that could help Paul Kraut Jr. realise his ambitious goals. In order to be able to retain Schleich's position as world leader in the toy figurine market, as well as to extend and cement this advantage, a change in personnel, coupled with a modern business strategy, was essential. In 2007, Paul Kraut Jr. invited Erich Schefold, an established financial expert, to become a managing director. He also bolstered his management team with marketing and technology specialists. Since then Kraut Jr. and Schefold have continued to hone the profile of the company, now known under Schleich GmbH. Some theme worlds have emerged from among the myriad of miniature animals that are not populated by zookeepers, but by knights, farmers, elves, and fantasy heroes. If we get the impression that imaginative play fills the manufacturers' hearts with as much joy as those of its customers, then that is no coincidence. The figures made at Schleich are more than just end products of a series of planning and work processes. Born from the imagination of their creators, they only really come alive during play.

Left and above
The animals of the *World of Nature* can turn the playroom into a rural landscape – or the savannah.

97

How is it that little children are so intelligent and men so stupid. It must be education that does it.

Alexandre Dumas, fils

With so many names, dates, and changing titles, it is not always easy to keep track of all the plot threads and stories, which, as in any comprehensive history, tend to become tangled into a tight ball. At the end of it all, it is only natural to ask oneself what has become of this or that person who played a role here or there in the story.

The company founder, Friedrich Schleich, died in 1978 at the age of 78. He left his entire fortune to a foundation for the benefit of the activities of the associations in Herlikofen. Since then, their presidents have been invited to the town hall every year, where they receive a generous check on behalf of their associations. Hermann Schneider, Friedrich Schleich's successor, resigned from the firm after the bankruptcy, but he maintained his links with the company to the end of his life as a consultant and an inspiring provider of ideas. Heinz Mehner, who at the time of the bankruptcy had to compile the list, as it was called, of redundancies for operational reasons, continued working for the company as production manager until 1999. As a native of the Erz Mountains it was a matter close to his heart to organise the cooperation between Schleich and a plastics manufacturer in the south of Saxony following reunification – a company which continues to manufacture accessories for the toy world to this day. Heidemarie Straube, who one Sunday suddenly found herself playing host to five Chinese guests, was director of purchasing until she retired in 2008, having worked not only with "Old Schleich" but with all his successors, too. She lives just a few steps away from the head office and still bakes delicious cakes. Wolfgang Brauer, once the best-dressed lorry driver in

Schleich in the twenty-first century:
catalogues from 2001 to 2010

Baden-Württemberg, no longer embarks on his business trips behind the wheel of a lorry. However, he probably still wears a suit and tie on his travels. Franz-Ulrich Köster, who retired in 2003, and was responsible for effectively steering the company through the post-bankruptcy period, making a significant contribution to its successful renaissance, now lives a few minutes from his old factory. Sometimes, when the afternoon peace of Herlikofen is shattered by the noise of a sports car, the staff in the Schleich offices nod to each other knowingly: it's Herr Köster again.

Eva Zippel, the firm's first model designer, resigned in 1976 and began to work for the city of Stuttgart, before eventually dedicating herself entirely to sculpting, which she pursued to a ripe old age. Jopo, the first and subsequently famous bendable figure, even received its own monument in 2004. A Dutch artist designed his sculpture according to the prototype of a "doll from the 1950s", which was unmistakably Jopo from Schwäbisch Gmünd.

And what became of the millions of Smurfs and their television colleagues Maya the Bee, Wum and Wendelin, or Lucky Luke? If you ask yourself or others this question, you will get to hear all sorts of stories and adventures – the starry-eyed memories of happy childhood days.

* More than seven million collector's booklets are printed in 27 languages.

Material test

Shipping

Attractive arrangement

Office corridor

Company premises

This publication is listed in the Deutsche Nationalbiblio-
grafie. Detailed bibliographic data are retrievable online
at http://dnb.ddb.de.

ISBN 978-3-86922-969-0

© 2010 by DOM publishers, Berlin (1ˢᵗ edition)
www.dom-publishers.com

DOM
publishers

Edited by
Paul Kraut, Erich Schefold

Author
Cornelia Dörries

Research
Ulrich Gohl

Translation
Tradukas GbR

Graphic design
Yuko Stier

Cover design
Gitte Brohl

Final artwork
Nicole Wolf

Credits
Bardon, Andres: 92, 94, 96; Heydiri, Beatrice: 24/25,
36/37, 60/61, 76/77, 86/87, 98/99; Hoch, Eberhard:
22, 23; Huthmacher, Werner: 110, 111; Studio Waldeck
(Christian Habermeier and Sebastian Jäger): 1–14, 85,
90, 102–110; Wolpert, Gerd: 40, 48, 56, 58, 64, 67,
70–75, 82–84, 93, 95, 97. All other images are from
the Schleich® company archives.

References
Unless stated otherwise, all quotations are from
the Schleich® company chronicles, compiled by
Ulrich Gohl in 2009–10. All Schleich® figurines produced since 1965 are listed in chronological order
in Der große Sammlerkatalog für Schleichtiere
(Ismaning, 2009).

Schleich Ⓢ   www.schleich-s.com

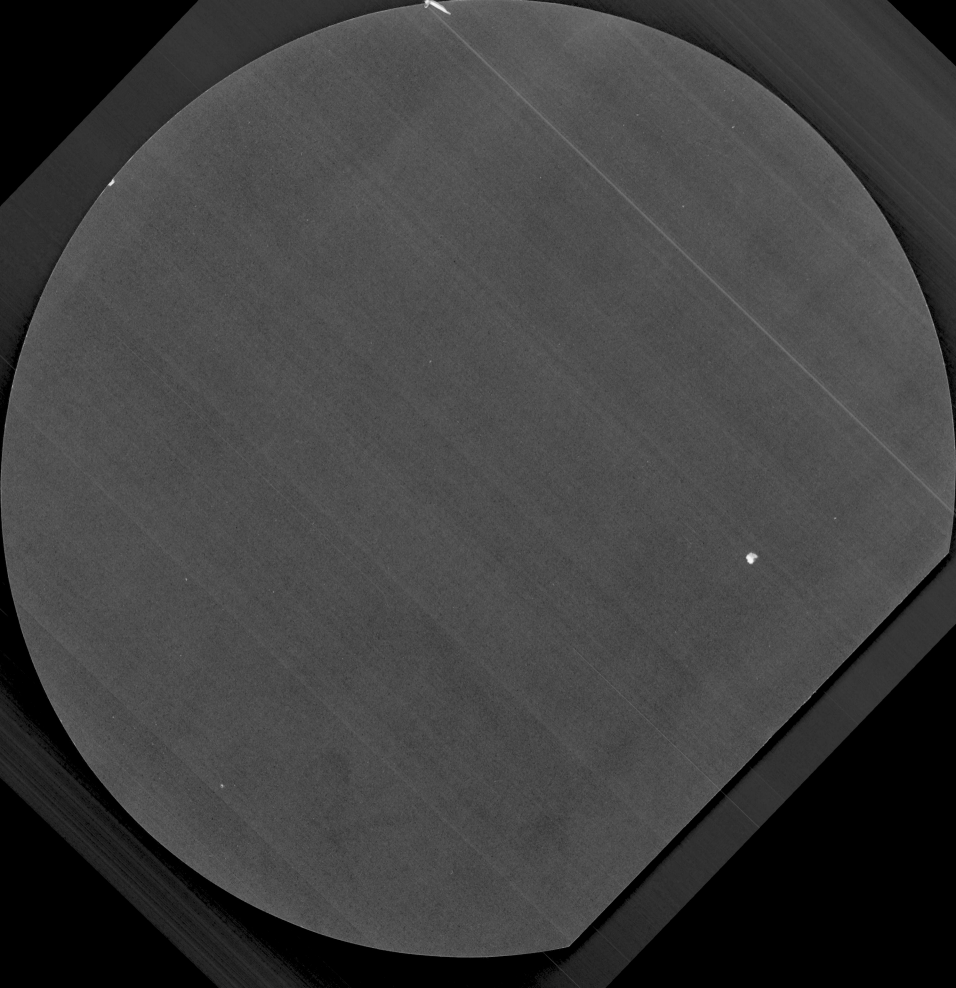